Investigating Accidents at Work: A Step-by-Step Guide to Safety and Industrial Hygiene

Table of Contents

Introduction

Workplace accidents, no matter how minor or severe, are signals that something has gone wrong in the system. Understanding the causes behind these incidents and learning from them is key to building a safer, more productive work environment. This e-book is designed as a practical, step-by-step guide to help safety officers, supervisors, and business owners effectively investigate accidents and implement improvements that promote industrial hygiene and risk management.

Chapter 1: Why Accident Investigation Matters

Accident investigations are a critical component of workplace safety and organizational responsibility. When an incident occurs, a thorough investigation does more than just document what happened—it uncovers underlying issues, drives corrective actions, and fosters a culture of safety. Below are the key reasons why accident investigations matter:

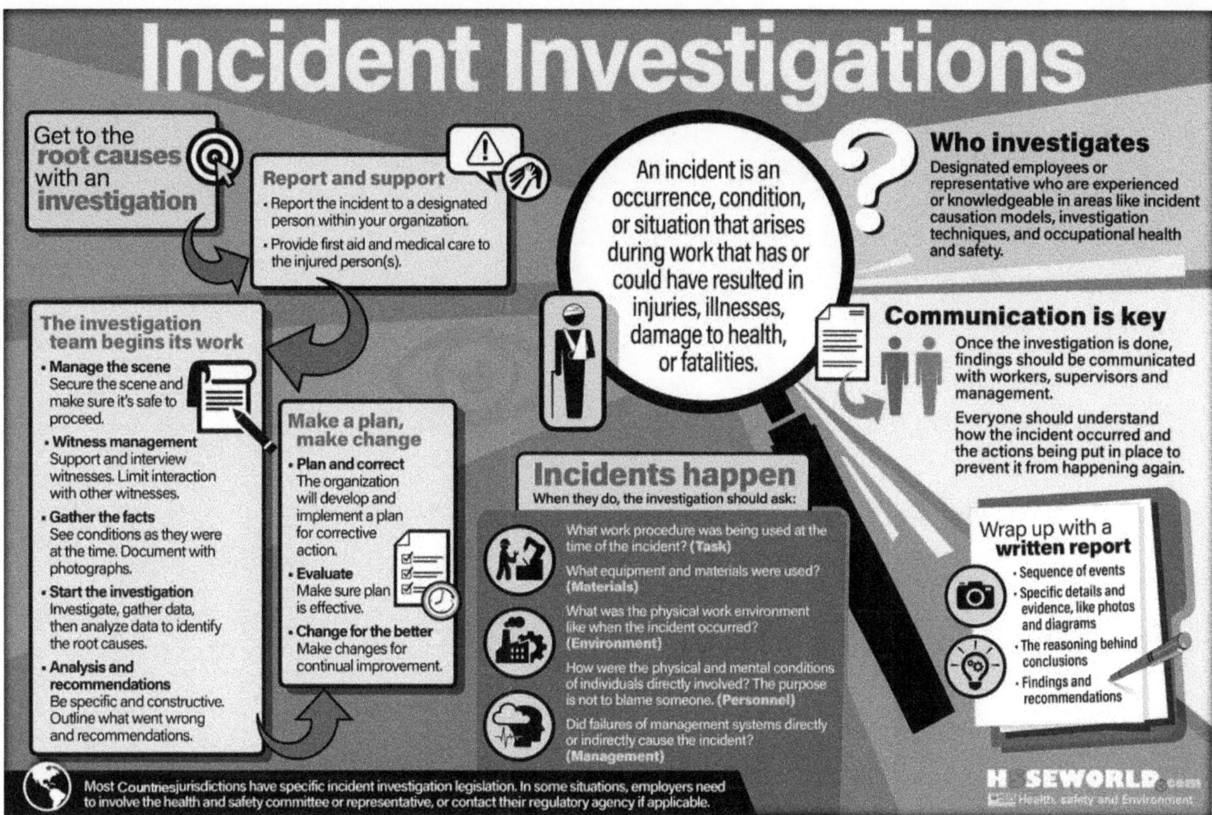

1. Uncovering Root Causes to Prevent Future Incidents

- Accidents are often symptoms of more profound problems, such as equipment failures, procedural gaps, or human error.
- A proper investigation identifies **root causes** (e.g., lack of training, poor maintenance, unsafe conditions) rather than just addressing surface-level symptoms.
- By implementing corrective actions, organizations can prevent similar incidents, improving long-term safety performance.

2. Ensuring Legal and Regulatory Compliance

- Many industries are governed by strict safety regulations (e.g., OSHA, ISO 45001, local labor laws).
- Proper investigations help organizations:
    - **Avoid penalties and fines** by demonstrating compliance with safety standards.

- **Provide necessary documentation** in case of legal disputes or regulatory audits.
- **Fulfill reporting obligations** for serious incidents, protecting the company from liability.

3. Supporting Insurance and Financial Protection

- Insurance claims often require detailed accident reports to determine liability and compensation.
- A well-documented investigation:
  - **Speeds up claims processing** by providing clear evidence.
  - **Reduces fraudulent claims** with factual, unbiased findings.
  - **Helps lower insurance premiums** by proving proactive risk management.

4. Demonstrating Commitment to Employee Safety

- Employees are more likely to follow safety protocols when they see that leadership takes incidents seriously.
- A transparent investigation process:
  - **Builds trust** between workers and management.
  - **Encourages reporting** of near-misses and hazards before they lead to accidents.
  - **Reinforces a safety-first culture**, improving morale and productivity.

5. Improving Operational Efficiency

- Investigating accidents often reveals inefficiencies in workflows, equipment, or training.
- Addressing these issues can lead to:
  - **There should be fewer work disruptions** due to injuries or equipment failures.
  - **There are cost savings from reduced downtime and workers'** Compensation claims.
  - **Better resource allocation** by targeting high-risk areas.

Chapter 2: Preparing for Incident Investigation

A well-prepared organization can respond to accidents swiftly and effectively, ensuring accurate findings and meaningful corrective actions. Proper preparation involves assembling the right team, setting up efficient reporting systems, equipping investigators with the right tools, and fostering a culture that prioritizes learning over blame.

1. Establish a Trained Accident Investigation Team

- **Select Qualified Investigators:**
  - Include members from safety, operations, HR, and (if applicable) union representatives.
  - Ensure they have training in **root cause analysis (RCA)**, interviewing techniques, and evidence collection.
- **Define Roles & Responsibilities:**
  - **Team Leader**—Oversees the investigation, ensures timelines are met.
  - **Evidence Collector**—Documents the scene (photos, measurements, samples).
  - **Interviewer**—Talks to witnesses and involved personnel.
  - **Analyst**—Identifies contributing factors and root causes.
- **Provide Ongoing Training:**

- There should be regular refreshers on investigation techniques, such as 5 Whys and Fishbone Diagrams.
- Mock drills to simulate real-world accident scenarios.

2. Maintain a Clear Reporting Process

- **Standardized Reporting Forms:**
  - Ensure all employees know how and where to report incidents (digital systems, paper forms, hotlines).
  - Include fields for date/time, **location, involved personnel, witness statements, and immediate actions taken.**
- **Immediate Notification Protocol:**
  - Define who must be notified (supervisors, safety team, management) and within what timeframe.
  - Use **automated alerts** (if applicable) to speed up response.
- **Near-Miss Reporting Encouragement:**
  - Train employees to report **near misses—these** can reveal hazards before an accident occurs.

3. Keep Necessary Tools Handy

- **Investigation Kit Checklist:**
  - **Documentation Tools:** Notebooks, pens, checklists, pre-formatted report templates.
  - **Evidence collection: a camera (or smartphone), measuring tape, and** sample containers (for spills or debris).
  - **Safety Gear:** PPE (gloves, goggles, hard hats) to protect investigators.
  - **Technology:** Tablets/laptops for digital reporting, voice recorders (with consent) for interviews.
- **Accessible Storage:**
  - Keep kits in **easily accessible locations** (e.g., safety office, supervisor stations).
  - Regularly check and restock supplies.

4. Foster a No-Blame Culture That Encourages Accurate Reporting

- **Emphasize Learning Over Punishment:**
  - Communicate that investigations aim to **improve systems**, not assign blame.

- Recognize employees who report hazards or near misses.
  - **Confidentiality & Psychological Safety:**
    - Assure witnesses that their statements will be used **only for safety improvements**.
    - Avoid retaliatory actions—employees who fear punishment may hide critical details.
  - **Leadership Commitment:**
    - Managers must **model accountability** by openly discussing incidents and corrective actions.
    - Reinforce that **safety is a shared responsibility**, not just a compliance requirement.

Chapter 3: Immediate Response to an Incident

The moments following an accident are critical—how an organization responds can **save lives, minimize harm, and ensure a successful investigation**. This chapter outlines the **priority actions** to take immediately after an incident occurs, focusing on **safety, medical care, reporting, and evidence preservation**.

1. Prioritize Immediate Response and Safety

A. Secure the Scene to Prevent Further Harm

- **Isolate the Area:**
  - Use barriers, cones, or caution tape to block access.
  - Stop any ongoing operations that could worsen the situation.
- **Assess Hazards:**
  - Check for **chemical spills, electrical hazards, fire risks, or structural damage**.
  - If the scene is unsafe (e.g., gas leak, unstable structure), evacuate and wait for experts.

B. Provide Medical Assistance to the Injured

- **First Aid & Emergency Care:**

- Follow **first-response protocols** (e.g., CPR, bleeding control, burn treatment).
  - Use onsite medical kits or call **emergency services (911/equivalent)** if needed.
- **Document Injuries:**
  - Note the **nature of injuries** (cuts, fractures, and chemical exposure) for later reporting.
  - If possible, ask injured personnel what happened **before memory fades**.

C. Report the Incident Without Delay

- **Internal Notification:**
  - Alert **supervisors, safety officers, and management** immediately.
  - Follow company **escalation protocols** (e.g., phone tree, emergency alert system).
- **Regulatory & Legal Reporting (if required):**
  - Some incidents (serious injuries, fatalities, major spills) must be reported to **OSHA, EPA, or other agencies** within **24–48 hours**.
  - Failure to report can lead to **fines or legal consequences**.

2. Preserve Evidence Early

Evidence degrades quickly—**documenting the scene before cleanup or alterations is crucial** for an accurate investigation.

A. Take Clear Photos & Videos

Earn a lifetime commission for every new bet slip service customer!

- **Capture:**
  - **The entire scene is captured in wide-angle shots.**
  - **Close-ups** of damaged equipment, tools, or hazardous conditions.
  - **Environmental factors include lighting, weather, and floor conditions.**
- **Best Practices:**
  - Use a **ruler or object for scale** in close-up images.
  - Time-stamp photos if possible.

B. Avoid Moving Items Unless Necessary for Safety

- **Do Not:**
    - Clean up spills, reposition machinery, or discard broken parts unless **absolutely necessary for safety**.
- **If Movement is Unavoidable:**
    - Document the **original position** (photos, sketches, notes) before moving anything.

C. Log Eyewitness Information Immediately

- **Gather Witnesses:**
    - Record **names, job roles, and contact details** of anyone who saw the incident.
    - Separate witnesses to **prevent discussion that alters memories**.
- **Initial Statements (If Possible):**
    - Ask **open-ended questions** (e.g., *"What did you see and hear?"*).
    - Avoid leading questions that suggest blame.

3. Additional Considerations

A. Assign a Scene Custodian

- Designate someone to **control access** and ensure no evidence is disturbed.

B. Document Time & Conditions

- Record:
    - **Exact time** of the incident.
    - **Consider the weather, lighting, and noise levels** (if relevant).

C. Begin a Chain of Custody for Evidence

- If one collects physical evidence (tools, samples),
    - Label it with **the date, time, collector's name, and location**.
    - Store securely to prevent tampering.

Chapter 4: Conducting a Thorough Investigation

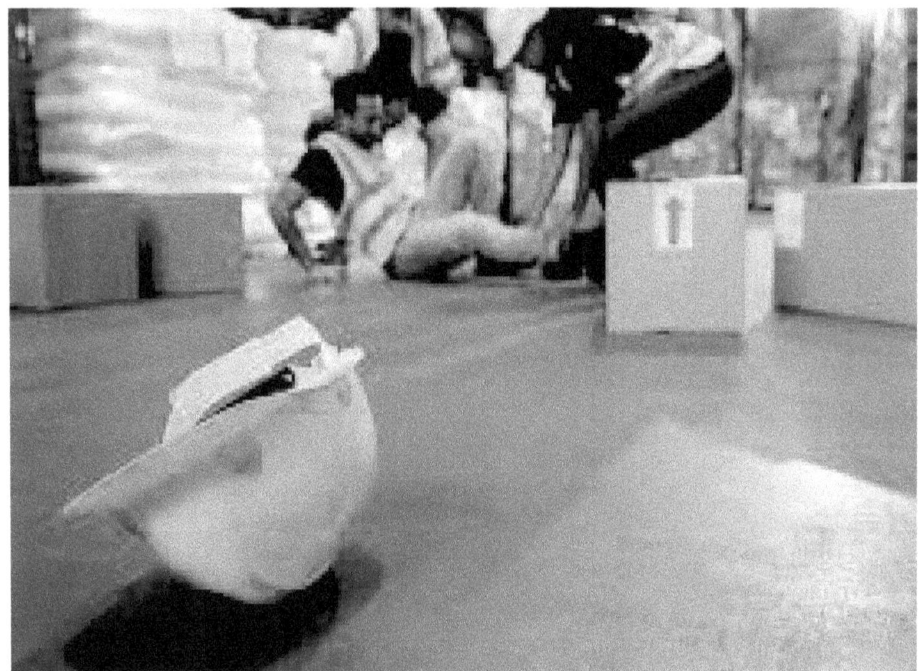

A proper accident investigation goes beyond just identifying what happened—it uncovers **why** it happened and **how** to prevent it from recurring. This chapter outlines a structured approach to **interviewing witnesses, documenting findings, and analyzing evidence** to determine root causes.

1. Conduct Thorough Interviews

Eyewitness accounts are critical, but human memory is fallible. Proper interviewing techniques ensure **accurate, unbiased information**.

A. Speak to All Witnesses Individually and in Private

- **Why?** Group discussions can lead to **memory contamination** (witnesses influencing each other).

- **Best Practices:**
    - Interview **as soon as possible** (memories fade quickly).
    - Choose a **quiet, neutral location** (avoid intimidating settings like a supervisor's office).
    - Ensure confidentiality to encourage honesty.

B. Ask Open-Ended Questions

- **Avoid Leading Questions:**
  "Did you see him ignore the safety guard?" (Suggests blame.)
  "What did you observe before the incident?" (Neutral, fact-finding.)
- **Effective Questioning Techniques:**
    - **5 Ws & H:**
        - *Who was involved?*
        - *What exactly happened?*
        - *When and where did it occur?*
        - *Why do you think it happened?*
        - *How could it have been prevented?*
    - **Clarify Without Judging:**
        - *"Can you walk me through what you saw step by step?"*

C. Remain Neutral and Avoid Assigning Blame

- **Psychological Safety Matters:**
    - If witnesses fear punishment, they may **withhold key details**.
    - Use **non-accusatory language** (e.g., *"We're trying to understand what went wrong to prevent future accidents."*).
- **Watch for Body Language:**
    - Hesitation, nervousness, or inconsistencies may indicate **missing information**.

2. Document Everything Clearly

Accurate documentation ensures **reliable analysis, legal defensibility, and corrective action tracking**.

A. Keep Detailed Notes of Observations & Interviews

- **What to Record:**
    - **Witness statements** (word-for-word when possible).
    - **The environmental conditions include lighting, weather, and equipment status.**
    - **The sequence of events refers to the timeline of actions that led to the incident.**
- **Best Practices:**
    - Use **a standardized incident report template**.
    - Sign and date all notes for credibility.

B. Use Sketches or Diagrams to Illustrate the Scene

- **Why?** Photos alone may miss spatial relationships.
- **How to Sketch Effectively:**
    - Include **measurements** (e.g., distance between machinery, spill size).
    - Label **key objects** (tools, hazards, and witness positions).

C. Maintain a Consistent Format for Record-Keeping

- **Benefits:**
    1. The system allows for easier **comparison** across multiple incidents.
    2. It simplifies regulatory audits and **internal reviews**.
- **Suggested Structure:**
    1. **The incident overview includes the date, time, and location.**
    2. **The list includes the names and roles of the personnel involved.**
    3. **The witness statements are direct quotes.**
    4. **The evidence log includes photos, diagrams, and samples.**
    5. **The preliminary findings were based on immediate observations.**

3. Additional Best Practices

A. Cross-Check Statements with Physical Evidence

- Example: If a witness says, *"The machine was making a strange noise,"* verify with:

  - Maintenance logs.
  - Please provide any available audio/video recordings.

B. Use Root Cause Analysis (RCA) Tools

- **5 Whys:** Keep asking *"Why?"* until the underlying cause is found.
- **Fishbone Diagram:** Visually map out contributing factors (people, equipment, methods, environment).

C. Hold a Preliminary Review Before Finalizing the Report

- Discuss findings with the **investigation team** to fill gaps or resolve contradictions.

Chapter 5: Root Cause Analysis

The key to preventing future accidents lies not in addressing **surface-level causes, but** in uncovering the **underlying systemic failures** that allowed the incident to occur. This chapter explores **structured root cause analysis (RCA) techniques** to move beyond blame and implement lasting solutions.

<u>Earn a lifetime commission for every new bet slip service customer!</u>

1. Why Root Cause Analysis Matters

- **Prevents Recurrence:** Fixing only the obvious cause (e.g., "worker slipped") ignores more profound issues (e.g., lack of anti-slip flooring, poor drainage).
- **Improves Systems:** RCA reveals **process flaws, training gaps, or design failures** that affect overall safety.
- **Reduces Blame Culture:** Focusing on **systems rather than individuals** encourages honest reporting.

2. How to Identify Root Causes

A. Use the 5 Whys Technique

Process: Keep asking *"Why?"* until you reach the fundamental cause.

Example:

1. **Why did the worker fall?** → The worker slipped on an oily patch.
2. **Why was there oil on the floor?** → A machine was leaking.
3. **Why was the machine leaking?** → A gasket was worn out.
4. **Why wasn't the gasket replaced?** → Maintenance checks were overdue.
5. **Why were checks overdue?** → No scheduled preventive maintenance system.

Root Cause: Lack of a preventive maintenance program.

Best Practices:

- Stop when the answer becomes **a process or policy failure** (not just human error).
- If multiple answers arise, investigate **all potential paths**.

B. Apply the Fishbone Diagram (Ishikawa)

A visual tool to categorize causes into **six key areas**:

1. **People** (Training, fatigue, supervision)
2. **Methods** (Procedures, work instructions)
3. **Machines** (Equipment failure, maintenance)
4. **Materials** (Defective parts, improper storage)
5. **Environment** (Lighting, temperature, noise)
6. **Management** (Policies, resource allocation)

How to Use It:

1. Draw the "fish bone," labeling each bone with a category.

2. Brainstorm possible factors under each.
3. Identify who contributed most to the incident.

Example:

- *A forklift collision could stem from:*
    - **People:** Untrained operator.
    - **Methods:** No clear traffic lanes.
    - **Machines:** Faulty brakes.
    - **Management:** No refresher training program.

C. Look Beyond Human Error

- **Human error is often a symptom, not a cause.** Ask:
    - Was the worker **properly trained**?
    - Were **safety guards missing**?
    - Were **procedures unclear**?
    - Was there **time pressure or fatigue**?
- **Example:**
    - *"Worker didn't wear gloves"* → Root cause may be:
        - Gloves not provided.
        - Gloves are uncomfortable (poor ergonomics).
        - No enforcement of PPE policies.

3. Avoiding Common RCA Pitfalls

Stopping Too Soon (e.g., blaming "carelessness" without probing deeper).

Assuming one cause (**most** accidents have **multiple contributing factors**).

Ignoring Organizational Factors (budget cuts, production pressures).

4. Turning Findings Into Action

After identifying root causes:

1. **Prioritize fixes** (which causes are most critical?).
2. **Assign Accountability** (Who will implement changes?).
3. **Track Progress: Verify solutions are effective.**

Chapter 6: Implementing Corrective Measures

Finding the core causes is just the first step; the successful execution of corrective actions guarantees genuine transformation. This chapter covers how to **develop, execute, and monitor** preventive measures while fostering a **no-blame safety culture.**

1. Recommend Preventive Actions

A. Suggest Practical, Measurable Solutions

Address root causes with **specific, actionable steps**:

Root Cause	Possible Corrective Measures
Lack of training	- Mandatory refresher courses - Hands-on competency assessments
Faulty equipment	- Scheduled maintenance checks - Red-tag system for defective tools

| **Poor lighting** | - Install additional fixtures |
| | - Routine inspection protocol |

| **Unclear procedures** | - Simplify work instructions |
| | - Visual aids (e.g., signage, diagrams) |

Key Criteria for Effective Actions:

✔ **Feasible** (cost, time, and resource-efficient).

✔ **Sustainable** (Not just a "quick fix").

✔ **Verifiable** (can be audited for compliance).

B. Assign Responsibilities & Deadlines

- Use a **tracking table** to ensure accountability:

Action Item	Responsible Person	Deadline	Status
Repair leaking valve	Maintenance Team	15/03/2025	In progress
Conduct safety training	HR Manager	30/03/2025	Pending

Tip: Integrate with digital tools (e.g., SharePoint, Trello) for real-time updates.

2. Encourage a No-Blame Culture

A. Promote Learning Over Punishment

- **Communicate Transparently:**
  - Share investigation findings company-wide (*"Here's what happened, and here's how we're fixing it"*).
  - Highlight **near-miss reports** as success stories (*"Thanks to Mark's alert, we prevented a potential injury"*).
- **Respond Constructively to Mistakes:**
  - Instead of: *"Why weren't you following the procedure?"*
  - Try: *"What made it hard to follow the procedure? How can we improve it?"*

B. Involve Employees in Solutions

- **Safety Committees:** Include frontline workers in brainstorming preventive measures.
- **Anonymous Feedback Channels:** Allow staff to report hazards without fear.

Signs of a Healthy Safety Culture:

- Employees **voluntarily report** near misses.
- Teams **collaborate on fixes** (e.g., suggesting better PPE designs).

3. Follow Up and Monitor Changes

A. Verify Implementation

- **Post-Action Checks:**
  - Revisit the incident site to confirm:
    - New guardrails installed.
    - Updated signage is visible.
  - Audit training records for completion.

B. Measure Effectiveness

- **Lagging Indicators:**
  - There has been a reduction in injury rates.

- ○ Fewer repeat incidents.
- **Leading Indicators:**
  - ○ There has been an increase in near-miss reports, which demonstrates trust in the system.
  - ○ There are higher PPE compliance rates.

C. Adjust as Needed

- **Example:**
  - ○ If workers ignore a new safety procedure, investigate:
    - Is it too time-consuming?
    - Was training inadequate?

Case Study: Turning Failure into Improvement

Incident: The failure to wear goggles resulted in a worker suffering chemical burns.

Root Cause: Goggles were uncomfortable; no enforcement.

Corrective Actions:

1. I have trialed three ergonomic goggle models with staff input.
2. I implemented mandatory PPE checks at the start of each shift.
3. We conduct quarterly "Safety Gear Comfort" surveys.
   Result: 100% compliance within 3 months; no repeat incidents.

Chapter 7: Documenting the Investigation

Proper documentation ensures that **investigation findings are clear, actionable, and defensible**—whether for internal improvement, regulatory compliance, or legal protection. This chapter provides **best practices for report writing** and includes a **customizable template** to standardize your process.

1. Why Documentation Matters

- **Legal & Regulatory Defense**—A well-documented report proves due diligence.
- **Knowledge Sharing**—Helps other teams learn from incidents.
- **Tracking Trends**—Identifies recurring issues across multiple investigations.

2. Key Elements of an Investigation Report

A. Standardized Template Structure

1. Incident Overview

- Date, time, location
- Personnel involved (names, roles)
- Type of incident (injury, near-miss, property damage)

2. Immediate Response Summary

- Actions taken (first aid, scene security)
- Initial observations

3. Investigation Methodology

- Who conducted the investigation?
- Tools used (5 Whys, Fishbone Diagram, interviews)

4. Findings & Evidence

- Witness statements (direct quotes)
- Photos, diagrams, lab reports
- Identified hazards (unsafe conditions/behaviors)

5. Root Cause Analysis

- Primary and contributing causes (use RCA tools from Chapter 5)

6. Corrective & Preventive Actions

- Specific fixes (training, equipment upgrades, policy changes)
- Responsible parties and deadlines

7. Follow-Up Plan

- How effectiveness will be measured (e.g., audits, KPIs)
- Scheduled review date

B. Simplified Report Template

[Your Company Logo]

INCIDENT INVESTIGATION REPORT

1. Basic Information

- **Report Number:** [Auto-generated]
- **Date of Incident:** [DD/MM/YYYY]
- **Location:** [Site/Department]
- **Report Prepared By:** [Name, Title]

2. Incident Description

- **What happened?** [Concise summary]
- **Severity:** [Minor injury, major injury, near-miss, etc.]

3. Investigation Details

- **Team Members:** [List names/titles]
- **Evidence Collected:**
  - Photos: [Yes/No] | Diagrams: [Yes/No] | Samples: [Yes/No]
- **Witnesses Interviewed:** [Names, roles]

4. Root Cause Analysis

- **Immediate Cause:** [E.g., "Worker slipped on wet floor."]
- **Underlying Causes:** [E.g., "No leak detection system"]
- **Root Cause:** [E.g., "Inadequate maintenance procedures"]

5. Recommended Actions

Action	Responsible Party	Due Date	Status
Install anti-slip mats	Facilities Manager	15/03/2015	Pending
Revise maintenance checklist	Safety Officer	30/03/2025	In Progress

6. Approval & Signatures

- **Investigator:** _________________ Date: //___
- **Safety Manager:** _______________ Date: //___

3. Best Practices for Documentation

A. Write Clearly & Objectively

- **Avoid:** *"John was careless."*
- **Use:** *"PPE was not worn; possible reasons include discomfort or lack of training."*

B. Attach Supporting Evidence

- Photos with timestamps.
- Witness statements (signed if possible).
- Maintenance records, training logs.

C. Store Reports Securely

- Digital archives with restricted access.
- Version control to track updates.

4. Example: Completed Report Snippet

Incident: Chemical spill in Lab B.

Root Cause:

- **Immediate:** Broken seal on storage drum.
- **Underlying:** No routine inspection of chemical containers.
- **Root:** Lack of written inspection protocol.
  Actions:
1. Implement weekly container checks (Lab Supervisor | Due: 20/02/2025).
2. Train staff on spill response (EHS Team | Due: 10/02/2025).

Chapter 8: Fostering a No-Blame Safety Culture

A **no-blame culture** is the foundation of effective safety management. When employees trust that reporting hazards and incidents won't lead to punishment, organizations gain **more accurate data, faster problem-solving, and proactive risk reduction**. This chapter explains how to build and sustain this culture.

1. Why a No-Blame Culture Matters

A. The Problem with Blame

- **Fear of reporting** → Hidden hazards → More severe accidents.
- **Surface-level fixes** (e.g., firing a "careless" worker) ignore **systemic causes** (poor training, faulty equipment).

B. The Benefits of No-Blame

✔ **More near-miss reports** (early warnings before injuries occur).

✔ **Deeper root cause analysis** (workers share honest insights).

✔ **Higher morale** (employees feel valued, not scapegoated).

2. How to Promote Learning Over Punishment

A. Leadership Commitment

- **What Leaders Should Do:**
    - Publicly endorse **"No retribution for reporting"** policies.
    - Share stories where **employee feedback prevented disasters**.
    - Replace *"Who messed up?"* with *"What failed, and how do we fix it?"*

B. Policy & Communication

1. **Formalize the Approach:**
    - Include **no-blame principles** in the safety handbook.
    - Train managers on **non-punitive response techniques**.
2. **Reinforce Through Actions:**
    - Recognize employees who **report hazards or near-misses**.
    - Celebrate **corrective actions taken** (not just "zero incidents").

C. Practical Steps for Investigators

- **Interviewing Without Blame:**
    - *"Why didn't you follow the procedure?"* (Accusatory)

- - "What made it difficult to follow the procedure?" (Problem-solving)
- **Reporting Language:**
    - Avoid: *"Worker failed to..."*
    - Use: *"The system did not ensure..."*

3. Addressing Resistance

A. Common Concerns & Responses

Objection	How to Respond
"Won't people take risks if there's no punishment?"	"Data shows punitive cultures have **more hidden incidents—no blame** encourages **early reporting**."
"How do we handle reckless behavior?"	"Gross negligence (e.g., willful violations) is still addressed—but **most errors stem from flawed systems**."

B. Balancing Accountability & Learning

- **Not "No Consequences," but "Fair Consequences":**
    - **System failure** → Fix the process.
    - **Repeated disregard for safety** → Coaching, then discipline.

4. Measuring Success

Track cultural progress with:

- **Leading Indicators:**
    - ↑ Near-miss reports.
    - ↑ Participation in safety committees.

- **Lagging Indicators:**
    - ↓ Repeat incidents.
    - ↓ Workers' comp claims.

Survey Employees Annually:

"Do you feel comfortable reporting safety concerns without fear of retaliation?"

Case Study: Aviation's "Just Culture" Model

- **Problem:** Pilots hid errors due to fear of license revocation.
- **Solution:** The FAA adopted **Just Culture**, distinguishing between:
    - **Human error requires training and system improvement.**
    - **The coach is exhibiting at-risk behavior.**
    - **It is important to avoid reckless actions and maintain discipline.**
- **Result:** 70% increase in voluntary incident reports, making air travel safer.

Conclusion: Transforming Investigations into a Safer Future

Workplace accident investigations are not just about **fulfilling regulatory requirements**—they are a **powerful catalyst for organizational growth**. When done correctly, they turn incidents into opportunities to:

✔ **Prevent recurrences** by addressing root causes, not just symptoms.

✔ **Boost operational efficiency** by eliminating hazards that slow productivity.

✔ **Strengthen safety culture** by fostering trust, transparency, and shared responsibility.

Key Takeaways for Lasting Impact

1. **Prioritize Prevention Over Blame**

- Focus on **systemic fixes** (training, equipment, and processes) rather than individual faults.
        - Encourage employees to report near-misses **without fear of punishment**.
2. **Investigate with Rigor, Act with Purpose**
        - Use structured methods (**5 Whys, Fishbone Diagrams**) to uncover true causes.
        - Implement **measurable corrective actions** with clear accountability.
3. **Turn Insights into Institutional Knowledge**
        - Document lessons learned and share them across teams.
        - Regularly review past incidents to **spot trends and prevent new risks**.
4. **Make Safety a Core Value, Not a Checklist**
        - Leaders must **model safety-first behavior** every day.
        - Celebrate improvements—not just "zero incidents," but **proactive risk reduction**.

Earn a lifetime commission for every new bet slip service customer!

Final Call to Action

Stay safe. Vigilance saves lives.

Investigate thoroughly. Dig deeper than the obvious.

Learn Constantly. Every incident is a teacher.

By embracing these principles, your organization won't just **respond to accidents**—it will **prevent them**, creating a workplace where employees thrive and operations run smoothly.

www.ingramcontent.com/pod-product-compliance
Lightning Source LLC
Chambersburg PA
CBHW040222110726
48005CB00019B/3115